SUNNYLEA

SUNNYLEA

A 1920s childhood
remembered by

JEAN METCALFE

Good wishes,
Jean Metcalfe.

MICHAEL JOSEPH

First published in Great Britain by
Michael Joseph Limited
44 Bedford Square, London WC1
1980

ISBN 0 7181 1923 1

Typeset by South Bucks Typesetters Ltd.
and printed and bound in Italy by Mondadori.

*Dedicated to Colin
who missed this part
of the story*

These are all small things remembered from the small world of my first seven years.

Looking back has been like lifting the front off an old doll's house and finding that all the smells and sounds and sensations of long ago are still there waiting to be taken out and recognised. But, of course, someone who is fifty years older notices the cobwebs and shadowy corners more than the child did. Hindsight keeps reminding me that the faded photograph people living in Sunnylea's safe circle were not dolls with happy smiles forever fixed on their faces.

There was *Uncle Tom* – the square peg in a rounded family, always putting himself where he felt he belonged – on the rim;

Father – loved by everyone but diminished by his need to be so;

My Grandparents – kept vigorous and alive by battling with each other, *'Nana'* with her sharp tongue, *'Papa'* with his silences;

Mother – shy but strong;

Aunt Norrie – dominant and artistic, her wit and intelligence locked in by circumstance;

And me – softened by the expectations of these six adults into a creature without corners.

Now that they are gone, time, in the end, has sharpened my edges. Even so, I have tried to draw the doll's-house happenings as they seemed to me then, without cobwebs or shadows.

Now that they are gone, I remember them all with love.

MARCH 1923

To Gwen and Joe Metcalfe
In Reigate,
Surrey
A Daughter—Jean

FATHER works for the Southern Railway in their Head Office at Waterloo Station. He loves his job because trains are his life. He can recognise rolling stock from its shadow on a wall. And his free season ticket in its celluloid holder allows us to live here where there are catkins and butterflies, away from London.

Mother is a self-effacing smiling lady who thinks that, outside her own home, everyone is better at everything than she is. Her dairymaid prettiness which Father carried in a sepia photograph through the war, is becoming contentedly plump so she has taken to salmon-pink corsets with laces. Now and again, when she has made sure that no one will be calling, they glow on the washing line like a bright cotton sunset and the bones creak in the wind.

WE live at Sunnylea with a blind to keep the sun off the front door and no lea to speak of except a back garden of phlox and golden rod and one gnarled Blenheim Orange apple tree. The tree is horizontal with age and every autumn sweetens our sour little patch with a bonus of lumpy, green, citrus-scented apples.

If we cut it down and let in the light, Father says he could grow as many flowers as the people on the other side of the hedge he is cutting. He props his shears into the privet as he contemplates the pinks and wallflowers he too could grow if it were not for the shade. But when Mother and I beg him not even to think of it, there is a look of relief on his face. He doesn't really enjoy gardening.

We have a cat called Billy, a downstairs lavatory and no bathroom.

MOTHER'S sister, Norrie, is married to Father's brother, Tom. They live next door to us at Grenville and are like another set of parents to me.

Tom works in a Southern Railway office too, but he is more interested in sums than trains. He adds up pages of figures so fast it has become his party trick.

He and Norrie are not at all alike. She likes making things, perfectly finished birthday cakes, dolls' clothes, embroidered runners for the sideboard, and does not mind how long it takes. Tom does everything at speed. We can tell when he is helping her with the washing-up by the sound of breaking crockery which clatters across the fence between the houses.

Theirs is a bigger house than ours, with a bathroom and a geyser, but they have no children.

SUNNYLEA and Grenville are both rented from Mother's cousin, Daisy. I call her Aunt. She lives down the road at Sydneyville which is named to commemorate her father, William Caffyn's Test Match triumphs in Australia.

She has a daughter, Peggy, whom I greatly admire because she is older then me and has fair hair. Sometimes I am allowed to play hide-and-seek in her garden with Peggy and her grown-up friends but I cannot see them over the raspberry canes and keep getting lost.

There is a drawing-room in Daisy's house, with fine-boned furniture and shelves of pale china, and she has a motor car.

FATHER is the only driver among the three households, so wherever Daisy's car goes, we go too. Today is Sunday. The glass was rising when we tapped the barometer this morning so we are off to spend the day by the sea. Father and Tom will sit in the front while Norrie, Daisy and Mother squeeze into the back. With the hood down, there is room for Peggy and me to sit on little wooden stools between our mothers' knees.

There are waterwings and paddling shoes in the 'dickey' at the back of the car, and towelling wraps like tents, which pull up on drawstrings round the neck, for modest dressing if we decide to bathe. We have Diabolo to play with on the beach and we are all wearing our best clothes.

SOMETIMES we go to Angmering, sometimes Rottingdean, sometimes Bognor; but no matter which destination, because it makes him feel as daring as Malcolm Campbell or a stunt man in a Harold Lloyd film, Father always chooses to go down Handcross Hill. It is steeply dangerous, this hill, bordered every summer Sunday with cars buried in hedges, their radiators still steaming, while St John Ambulancemen wait hopefully in the valley below. By some miracle, Daisy's Bullnose Morris never founders. We arrive at the seaside intact, white stockings unblemished, hats in place, the men's suits still buttoned.

This Sunday we are at Bognor with sunshades for everyone and bathing caps like flying helmets. Peggy has a rubber mop cap to keep her hair dry. I am wearing my sun bonnet and mackintosh paddlers which keep more water in than out, and squelch when I move.

RETURNING home from an outing like this, we can never resist the Stop-Me-and-Buy-One sign on an ice cream man's tricycle. Penny Snofrutes are our favourites. Made of crumbly yellow, green or pink water ice, you have to push the stick of frozen syrup up through its check paper wrapper in order to bite bits off with tingling teeth. The last inch always tastes of cardboard and trickles sticky coloured water up your sleeve.

Tom is not a man for standing around doing nothing, so whenever these diversions occur, he is impatient to get the car going again, cranking the starting handle while Father sits languidly at the wheel.

THIS is 1926. Father loves the new crossword puzzles in his *Daily Express* and Mother enjoys whist drives in the church hall. But for me these are the daisy-chain days of painted wooden toys and stuffed dolls.

I have . . .

A push-along Felix the Cat

A pull-along Bonzo Dog

A Sunny Jim rag doll for which we saved the tops of Force cereal packets

And a wind-up, blue tin gramophone, made in Japan, which plays a very small record of 'When the Red, Red Robin Comes Bob, Bob, Bobbin' Along'.

MOST loved of all is my doll, Peggy, named after my idolised cousin, of course. She has corn-coloured *real* hair so firmly rooted that I can brush and comb it like my own. Unlike mine, which is stick straight and ginger, hers ripples with waves and curls. She has blue painted eyes which seem to twinkle, dimples to give her an impish expression and a 'skin' of warm peachy felt.

The only improvement I could wish for her is 'buck' teeth. I try to make mine project by biting my bottom lip in the daytime and praying for them at night . . . 'God bless Mummy and Daddy, Auntie and Uncle, Nana and Papa, and please make my teeth stick out in front.'

IN a house without a bathroom, the scullery has to be a number of things—kitchen, bathroom and wash-house in one. Father strops his safety razor beside Mother's baking tins and washboard. Ordinarily it is a dingy, damp-smelling place but, once a week, bath night transforms it into a cave of whispering gas-jets, shadows and steam. Mother fetches the hip-bath from the nail outside by the coal cellar and sets it down where we can feel the warm breath of the oven. Then she fills it with jugs of hot water while clean night clothes air on the clothes-horse.

On bath night, it is the treat of the week for her to tell me the story of a film she has seen. 'This man Ben Hur's chariot was faster than the other ones, you see . . .' or 'Abe's family don't want him to marry this girl called Rose because he's Jewish and she's an Irish Catholic.' What's Jewish? What's Catholic? Who is Ramon Navarro? My education begins with Hollywood in a hip-bath.

THIS is the scullery when it's being a wash-house—not the regular Monday scrubbing of underclothes and pinafores but the Big Wash Day, chosen because it is good drying weather and Mrs Durham is able to come and lend a hand. We haven't much money to spare but Mrs Durham has less because her husband is unemployed. With her she brings her handsome son, Frankie, who has hair like carved and polished mahogany. While our mothers work inside, Frankie and I are blowing bubbles with clay pipes and a bowl of Sunlight soapy water on the doorstep.

On washing day, the scullery is no place for children. There is a hot black flat-iron on its stand, a mangle which gobbles fingers and spits them back crushed and bruised, and a scalding boiler of handkerchiefs seething on the stove.

THE days are drawing in now and I go to bed by candlelight, but downstairs in the front room Father and Tom have been putting the finishing touches to a cat's-whisker radio they've been making. Five shillings it cost. A moment ago they called up the stairs, 'Come quickly and you can hear a man singing from a long way off.' The headphones are too big for me so I hold them over my ears while someone says, 'Keep very still and Uncle will adjust the whisker on the crystal.' The sea-shell hissing and crackling stops, and there it is—a man's voice, deep and muffled, sounding like Father Christmas inside a chimney. 'Think of it,' says Mother, 'now you can say you've actually heard Peter Dawson.'

I think they're disappointed because I'm not as excited as they are, but I like Mother's music better. We have a walnut piano with brass candle-holders on the front. She doesn't play very well but her voice is light and pretty when she sings my favourites, 'There are Fairies at the Bottom of my Garden' and 'Little Grey Home in the West'.

TO be ever so slightly ill is indolent bliss. For a day or two nobody tells you to put on your mac and muffler and go out in the 'lovely fresh air'. Nobody tells you to do anything except stay where you are and keep warm, with sugar-sprinkled bread and milk, raspberry vinegar to 'cut' a cough or a salt bag to soothe an aching ear.

Because ear-ache is my speciality, Mother is a salt bag expert. They are made like bean bags out of bits of old sheet, filled with cooking salt, then heated gently in the oven. Holding one against a throbbing ear is like cuddling a sleeping kitten.

When she has drawn the curtains at teatime, Mother fishes up the chimney with a poker to remove the sooty stuffing of birds' nests and paper, and lights a fire in the bedroom grate.

A coal fire in the bedroom, Father reading *Peter Pan* to me when he comes home from the office, and then, to fall asleep watching the fireguard throw a net of shadows over the room . . . this is better than a birthday.

MOTHER and Father are still young although they seem as old as rocks to me. In the summer, they play tennis on the bumpy, daisied courts behind the church, but when winter comes both Metcalfe families go to football on Saturdays. Because Redhill is playing away this week at a ground the other side of Croydon, we have to make the journey on the swaying open top of a bus.

A waterproof bib hangs from the back of each seat to tuck over your knees and catch a lapful of puddles when it rains. Leaning over the side, trying to touch lamp posts as we pass, I pretend to be in a boat. Even the conductor swinging on the open staircase at the back and tugging ting-ting on his bell-pull reminds me of a sailor on last summer's Weymouth pleasure-steamer.

I AM muffled to the eyes against germs and chills in a hated hairy scarf which is soon wet inside with condensed breath and dribble. Father has brought *Tiger Tim* and *Rainbow* and a 'Rupert' colouring book to occupy me while he watches the game. Once, when I broke all my pencils during a match, Father found he had left his penknife at home so in desperation he sharpened one for me with his teeth. I was enthralled. Today, to my disappointment, he has come well prepared with things to keep me happy in the stand. But I am not happy. With chapped cheeks and little attention, I am fed up.

When the match is over, with a bit of luck and expert grizzling, Father and Tom will be persuaded to take turns providing piggybacks and bandy chairs back to the bus stop, and later Mother may give us dripping toast for tea.

HAVING raised nine children, four girls and five boys including Father and Tom, it's not surprising that my Metcalfe grandparents are radiantly eccentric and go-as-you-please. They live in an old railway coach on a piece of New Forest land in Hampshire, too far away for us to see them more than once a year. Instead of the commonplace mice and sparrows most people have around their houses, Grandpa and Grandma Metcalfe have donkeys and ponies, nameless cats sleeping on the old train's buffers, chickens and turkeys, and a bounding hearthrug of a sheepdog called Woolly Bear.

Grandma has a soft spot for motor bikes, Chinese lanterns and tipsy trifle with marshmallows floating in the custard. She grows begonias as big as tea plates and, when the waxy flower heads fall, I float them in the water-butt like waterlilies.

WE could tell today was going to be a special occasion when Grandma put on her best stockings this morning—handknitted with a lacy pattern. When she stays at home, an old jacket of Grandpa's and a pair of gum boots is sufficient as often as not. Even her teeth are kept for the benefit of visitors. But on Salisbury Market Day, she looks like a duchess and is treated like one. In the Kardomah café, the manager is deferential, stall-holders know her by name. The Red Indian Medicine Man selling his 'magic elixir' pauses to ask after Grandpa, and the knife-grinder stops making sparks to shake her hand. I have to admit Grandma Metcalfe has style.

After walking round the booths of crockery and cretonne, bric-à-brac and boot polish, suddenly, without warning, we come upon a drover lifting pigs by their ears. Their squeals sound like screams to me, as terrible as torture. Grandma, the countrywoman for whom all Sunday dinners start with 'first catch your fowl', throws back her head in amusement. 'Don't worry, child,' she says, 'they like it. Listen to them laughing.'

MY Reed Grandparents—I call them 'Nana' and 'Papa' are, by comparison, both 'safe' and 'sound'. Or perhaps they just seem unexceptional because they live near enough to spend much of their time with us. Their house in Balham has venetian blinds, iron railings and a doorstep which is hearthstoned by Mrs Townroe, the charlady.

Nana's kingdom is the kitchen, any kitchen. She learnt to cook as a young governess in France and still keeps wine vinegar in the pottery jar she brought home with her when she married Papa.

More fascinating to me than her cooking is Nana's toilette. She wears her hair like Queen Alexandra, the back coiled on top with tortoiseshell pins, the front frizzed into a fringe with curling tongs which she heats over a small spirit stove. I love the smell of singeing tissue paper and the toast-coloured ridges the tongs make when she tests them for heat.

Cut-glass pots with silver lids hold her hairnets and pins, and a bonnet-brush to clean her hat hangs beside the looking-glass. There's a buttonhook to fasten her boots, a lace modesty vest to tuck in the neck of her dress and leaves of *papier poudre* to rub over her skin and bloom it like a freshly picked grape.

On the bamboo table by her bed, Nana keeps her inner needs— Carter's Little Liver Pills, Cascara Segrada, and barley water, brewed every day, under its muslin cover edged with beads.

[42]

I HAVE never seen Grandfather Reed without a fobbed watch chain looped across his waistcoat. He has small dapper feet and he always wears spats.

When Papa and his brother Walter were boys, it is said they were wild enough to whitewash the old Town Hall in the centre of Reigate on Mafeking night. But after Walter emigrated to the United States, Willie settled down to be solid and thrifty. At twelve he went to work as a barber's lather boy and now he has his own hairdressing premises in Jermyn Street where he dispenses pots of pommade for titled gentlemen and transformations of extra hair for their ladies.

Like a gardener with his secateurs, Papa never goes anywhere without his Gladstone bag of scissors, combs and clippers. Even on a brief visit to his daughters, we are all expected to have our hair cut, no matter how short it is already.

Norrie spreads a sheet on her kitchen floor and there, with towels round our necks, we wait to be shorn. It is a miserable business carried out in silence except for Papa's puffing concentration, the scalp brushed hard as if in punishment and, worst of all, the *coup de grâce* with clippers which tweak the smallest hairs on the back of the neck and leave it hot, sore and prickly for the rest of the day.

I wonder why the aristocracy in London is willing to pay for such torment, unless, like us, they don't like to hurt his feelings.

MY first fancy dress. I am a butterfly. There is going to be a children's party at Papa's Constitutional Club in Balham and everyone has to be dressed up. Norrie has bought some remnants in the Sales to make me a costume, silver metallic material and white net, so—I am a butterfly.

Norrie was an apprentice milliner and can conjure wonderful shapes out of wire and buckram. The frills of the skirt are made of net bound with the same silver material as the bodice. She's even made a smaller butterfly like the one on the headband, to wear on elastic round my finger. The metallic stuff is cold and sharp on the skin, but if I keep my vest on it shows round the neck and armholes. And anyway, butterflies don't wear vests.

The party is held in the Constitutional Club ballroom which has been french-chalked to an ice-rink gloss. We spend more time sliding on our white party knickers than playing the organised Musical Chairs and Nuts-in-May. Presently we have to march round in our costumes while the band plays 'The Policeman's Holiday', and I fall in love with the drummer because he winks at me.

Next year, Norrie says, she will make an even better fancy dress.

Next year, Papa will be on the Committee.

Next year, we shall win a prize.

FOR the first time, I am staying with Nana and Papa in Balham on my own. Their house in Hearnville Road is opposite a school which, to someone whose schooldays have not yet begun, makes mysterious and threatening noises. Through its open windows, the sound of chanted multiplication tables floats across the road. A bell rings, desk lids slam and the starling children come screaming out of school. I watch them from the safety of Nana's front railings as they wheel about the road bowling hoops and whipping tops—hard children playing hard games.

Nana spreads warnings round me like quicksands . . . 'Never buy from the muffin man. He keeps them under the bed', 'Don't touch the organ-grinder's monkey because of fleas', 'Lavatory seats are nasty', 'Bracken is full of adders' . . . But she is joyously rash when it comes to filling our afternoons. We go to Pike's Picture Palace in the High Road. True, we suck antiseptic lozenges all through the programme but she is entirely unconcerned about what we see. I have nightmares for weeks after seeing Rin Tin Tin plunge into a burning building while the projectionist floods the screen with flickering red light. And as for all those poor *Titanic* passengers, singing 'Nearer My God To Thee' while the sea creeps over their Lloyd Loom chairs . . . I shall never feel the same about Bognor again.

THE end of 1927—a white, white winter. Snow has been falling since Christmas. Every morning there is a frost on my bedroom window and a layer of ice on the water in the wash-stand jug. Our stone hot water bottles have not been put away since November. Nasty, vicious things, these stone hot water bottles, hot as griddles or cold as kerbstones and always as toe-stubbing hard as a boulder in the bed.

Every child who has one is wearing a Liberty Bodice. Mine has been outgrown by several before me. It has been washed so often, the white wool and ribbons have turned butter-yellow.

The Co-Op has sold out of ladies' leggings and men's goloshes and Mr Collier says he's never had so many skating boots to mend in all his years as a cobbler. Since New Year's Day, the ice on Priory Lake has been thick enough to bear, and on Breakneck Hill, where we go tobogganing, the snow has packed into a glacier as smooth as pulled toffee.

Tom has lost his garnet ring inside the snowman. We wonder if we'll find it when the thaw comes.

[50]

AS I shall be five years old tomorrow, Norrie and Tom have decided I am old enough to be taken to London for a birthday treat. We have been to see the pantomime *Puss In Boots* at the Lyceum in the Strand and now we're having tea at Lyons' Corner House: Tomato Soup and Poached Egg on Toast—9d.

The Corner House is like a cathedral—stained glass, marble pillars, 'In a Monastery Garden' played very quietly—so I behave beautifully as though I am in church. I shall always remember and envy the black-stockinged Nippies who wait at the tables with rows of tiny pearl buttons trimming the fronts of their dresses and bill pads and pencils swinging from dog-clips at their waists.

GOOD Friday. The men have not had to go to the office. With Peggy and Aunt Daisy, we are primrosing at Gadbrook where the wild cherry is in bloom in the hazel copse. There are dog violets and wood anemones among the cushions of primroses and lumps of lime-green sunlight lying in the grass.

This evening, we shall keep the flowers cool on the floor of the larder because Norrie needs them tomorrow to decorate the church for Easter. Every year she trims the pulpit with bunches of primroses tucked into hidden pots of water which are tied on with a network of string. We always save our empty fish-paste pots for Easter.

IT'S June, scorching and still, streets deserted because of the heat, tar melting on the roads. A friend who grows strawberries has given us some for tea and I have been allowed out on my own to buy a tuppenny carton of cream to go with them from Mr Risbridger's dairy.

His size must have something to do with my fondness for Mr Risbridger. He is only twice as tall as I am and has to reach up to the top of his shop counter. When he is out on his rounds, the milk cart almost obscures him from the front and looks as though it is running on its own. His hats too are exceptionally interesting. Sometimes he wears a bowler, sometimes an undulating panama, but always they appear to be screwed into the sunburnt lines on his forehead like the cap on the top of a Camp coffee bottle.

TODAY is Carnival Day. Lucky programmes have been on sale for weeks and we have flattened our noses against every shop front in the High Street trying to win the Carnival 'Odd One Out' competition—something hidden in a window display which the shop doesn't sell. Things like an O'Cedar mop with corsets hung over it in the draper's, and the box of pink plate powder we spotted beside a sweet shop's sherbert dabs.

The Carnival raises money for the East Surrey Hospital. I was there last year to have my tonsils out and I cried so much the Ward Sister had to ask Mother to take me home in order to spare the other patients. I was not a good girl. They told me there would be ice cream but not about the rubber sheets, sick bowls and dark green paint. Now, as the procession passes, Father has hitched me on to his shoulder ready to drop pennies into the fireman's collecting net—so that the hospital can buy more rubber sheets, sick bowls and dark green paint.

That is Mr Burtenshaw's lorry under the bunting and plywood coming round the corner. Father says the boat on top is meant to be the *Majestic* which is the biggest liner in the world. I am very taken with the lady wearing Prince of Wales feathers in her hair. According to Mother that is how posh people dress when they are presented at Court to the King and Queen. And there's the Town Band, bobbing along behind Britannia in a haycart.

IT is 1930 and the writing's on the wall for Sunnylea. Aunt Daisy and my parents have gone halves on the cost of electrifying our house without a bathroom. There are light bulbs in the cupboard under the stairs where the gas mantles used to be. The bright new light makes the whole house look like a jumble sale, says Mother, and wouldn't I like some nice new paint in my back bedroom? Ungrateful child, all I can do is wail. How can I explain?

For the first time in my life everything is changing. I go to school. Billy the cat has died. Without those dear old damp patches on my ceiling nothing will ever seem the same again. Father and Mother smile indulgently and let the shabby ceiling stay. But then, they know other changes are on the way which no amount of wheedling tears can alter.

Someone else, with baby fists, is about to push me from the centre of the picture. Not before time. Like it or not, soon I shall be an only child no longer, because . . .

JUNE 1930

To Gwen and Joe Metcalfe

In Reigate, Surrey

A Son—Colin

A Brother for Jean